What You Don't Know about Turning 50...

A Funny Birthday Quiz

P. D. Witte

Meadowbrook Press
Distributed by Simon & Schuster
New York

Library of Congress Cataloging-in-Publication Data
Witte, P. D. (Phil D.)
    What you don't know about turning 50—: a funny birthday quiz / P.D. Witte
        p. cm.
    ISBN: 978-0-88166-342-6 (Meadowbrook Press) ISBN 978-0-671-31773-7 (Simon & Schuster)
    1. Middle age Humor. 2. Middle-aged persons Humor. I. Title.
PN6231.M47W58 1999
818'.5402—dc21   99-37056
                                                  CIP

Editorial Coordinator: Joseph Gredler
Production Manager: Joe Gagne
Desktop Publishing: Danielle White
Illustrator: Steve Mark

Published by Meadowbrook Press, 6110 Blue Circle Drive, Suite 237, MN 55343
www.meadowbrookpress.com

BOOK TRADE DISTRIBUTION by Simon and Schuster, a division of Simon and Schuster, Inc.,
1230 Avenue of the Americas, New York, New York 10020

17 16 15 14   24 23 22 21 20 19 18 17 16

Printed in the United States of America

Contents

Chapter 1

Romance and Sex

Q: If women reach their sexual peak at age 40, when do men reach their sexual peak?

A: *During Baywatch.*

Q: Where can women over the age of 50 find young, sexy men who are interested in them?

A: *Try a bookstore, under fiction.*

Q: Losing one's virginity can be exhilarating, terrifying, and painful, but ultimately a big relief. Is there a similar experience for 50-year-olds?

A: *Yes: passing a kidney stone.*

Q: A lot of pro basketball players have shaved their heads. Doesn't that prove that baldness is sexy?

A: *Absolutely—and its effect on women may be intensified if you're also under 30, over 6-feet-6, incredibly athletic, and wealthier than many Eastern European nations.*

Q: What sort of people show up at a mixer for singles over 50?

A: *People over 60.*

Q: What's the most insulting word to describe a 50-year-old man's flirtations?

A: *Harmless.*

Q: When you're 50, is there a large mental component to sex?

A: *Yes, especially if your sex life consists mostly of fond memories.*

Q: What do men and women over 50 do to get down and dirty?

A: *They take up gardening.*

Q: Do 50-year-old men ever get "the seven-year itch"?

A: *Yes, but there are many effective medications available over the counter.*

Q: Why is a failed romance more painful for people over 50?

A: *You wake up with an aching heart and an aching back.*

Q: Can a 50-year-old woman be a femme fatale?

A: *Yes, if she marries an 80-year-old man with a heart condition.*

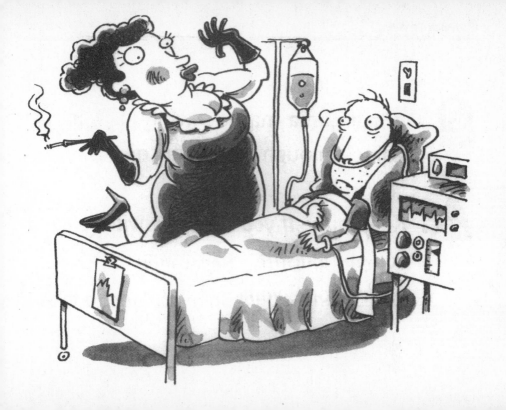

Q: What can a man do while his wife is going through menopause?

A: *Keep busy. If you're handy with tools, you can finish the basement. When you're done, you'll have a place to live.*

Chapter 2

Health and Medicine

Q: How can you increase the heart rate of your 50-year-old husband?

A: *Tell him you're pregnant.*

Q: How has the diet of today's 50-year-olds changed from the previous generation?

A: *Less brandy, more bran.*

Q: What repetitive stress-related disorder are 50-year-olds prone to?

A: *La-Z-Boy elbow.*

Q: What does it mean when every time you bite into something hard, you break a tooth?

A: *You are headed for a complete dental breakdown.*

Q: Are there certain foods that 50-year-olds shouldn't eat?

A: *Yes. Avoid any food that is spicy, salty, fried, fattening, creamy, meaty, filling, satisfying, or delicious.*

Q: When 50-year-olds do spring housecleaning, what's the one thing they're most likely to throw out?

A: *Their backs.*

Q: Is a person's sense of hearing less acute at age 50?

A: *Not at all. It's just that other people mumble more than they used to.*

Q: Is there anything wrong with a 50-year-old man taking up cigar smoking?

A: *Driving a red sports car would be a more subtle form of compensation.*

Q: What is a seven-course meal for 50-year-olds?

A: *Appetizer, entrée, dessert, and four types of vitamins.*

Q: Is 50 too young to be thinking about false teeth?

A: *You can cross that bridge when you get to it.*

Q: Why are 50-year-olds more stable than young people?

A: *They have a lower center of gravity.*

Q: Is 50 too young to be worried about bladder control problems?

A: *Depends.*

Chapter 3

Aging

Q: When is it time to buy bifocals?

A: *When your arms aren't long enough for you to read a book.*

Q: What is the next word in this sequence: Microsoft, Intel, Apple, _____?

A: *Fixodent.*

Q: What's in the Fountain of Youth?

A: *A mixture of Retin-A, minoxidil, and Viagra.*

Q: How can you avoid spotting a new wrinkle every time you walk past a mirror?

A: *The next time you're in front of a mirror, take off your glasses.*

Q: What does a 50-year-old woman have in common with a perspiring exhibitionist?

A: *Both are prone to hot flashes.*

Q: Some middle-aged people hear the voices of their parents when speaking to their own kids. Is there anything they can do about that?

A: *They should consider moving out of their parents' houses.*

Q: Midlife crisis is a lot of hogwash, right?

A: *Roll down the window of your Ferrari, and we'll explain it to you.*

Q: What do you call a 50-year-old man with no gray hair?

A: *Bald.*

Q: When can playing cards be depressing for 50-year-olds?

A: *When they realize that the Old Maid looks younger than they do.*

Q: What is the most frequently asked question among people age 50 and over?

A: *"Now what was I about to say?"*

Q: How do you cheer up a 50-year-old who's feeling his age?

A: *Remind him that Mickey Mouse is far older than he is.*

Q: What does it mean that a woman
is "of a certain age"?

A: *That one does not ask the woman
certain questions.*

Q: What is the most frequently asked question among people age 50 and over?

A: *You just asked that question a few pages ago. That's okay.*

Q: Why is 50 considered an awkward age?

A: *It's too old to rock and roll, but too young to demand a senior discount.*

Q: How can people tell when they've entered their autumn years?

A: *Their shadows are wider.*

Q: What does it mean to grow old gracefully?

A: *Having a toupee like Fred Astaire's or a face-lift like Ginger Rogers's.*

Q: How can a 50-year-old avoid admitting her age and still be truthful?

A: *Tell people you're 39 in tortoise years.*

Q: How does a 50-year-old stay young at heart?

A: *Keep doing the things that cause your children to say, "Stop it—you're embarrassing me!"*

Q: How can a mature woman avoid giving away her age in conversation?

A: *Don't use the words "Hummel figures" and "adorable" in the same sentence.*

Q: Does an adult's working vocabulary increase or decrease with age?

A: *Increase. The average 50-year-old can spell and define such difficult words as "analgesic," "sciatica," and "dyspepsia."*

Q: At 50, is it normal for a person to have lower expectations?

A: *Yes. For example, a young person may dream of conquering the world, while a 50-year-old may be satisfied with conquering the Mexican combo platter.*

Q: Why should 50-year-old people use valet parking?

A: *Valets don't forget where they parked your car.*

Q: How do you make a 50-year-old feel his age?

A: *Ask him to be part of an oral history project.*

Q: How does shopping for a car change as you get older?

A: *You're less concerned about gas mileage and more interested in lumbar support.*

59

Q: Is it common for 50-year-olds to
have problems with short-term
memory storage?

A: *Storing memory is not a problem.
Retrieving it is a problem.*

Q: As people age, do they sleep more soundly?

A: *Yes, but usually in the afternoon.*

Q: What happened to "If it feels good, do it"?

A: *It became "If you feel something pop, don't do it."*

Q: Does middle age begin at 50?

A: *Only if you believe that old age begins at 100.*

Q: Is it true that a fairly large percentage of men actually get thinner as they approach age 50?

A: *Only on top.*

Q: What gets shorter as people age?

A: *The intervals between birthdays.*

Q: When do 50-year-old parents experience the empty-nest syndrome?

A: *When they realize that their children's expenses have eaten up their nest egg.*

Chapter 4

Fashion

Q: Is there anything wrong with a 50-year-old wearing a bikini?

A: *Please take that off, sir.*

Q: What is the number one fashion "don't" for 50-year-old women?

A: *Kleenex up the sleeve.*

Q: Any rules for casual attire?

A: *Your closet should not contain more than three jogging suits, especially if you don't jog.*

71

Q: Does it look all right for an adult man to wear socks, sandals, and shorts?

A: *Such a man is sporting the "full dad" look. For the "full grandpa," substitute black dress shoes for sandals.*

Q: When is it time to update the 50-year-old's wardrobe?

A: *When trick-or-treaters wear costumes that resemble some of your casual wear.*

Q: What is the most common type of
body piercing for 50-year-olds?

A: *Accidentally sitting on a fishhook.*

Q: What is a versatile style of slacks for 50-year-olds?

A: *Anything with an elastic waistband.*

Q: Should the wardrobe of a 50-year-old woman include "the little black dress"?

A: *Yes: preferably two of them, so that they can be sewn into one big black dress.*

Q: Can a 50-year-old woman look good in Spandex?

A: *That's stretching it.*

Q: What do you call a 50-year-old who can tie a perfect bow tie every time?

A: *A wife.*

Q: What can a 50-year-old woman wear that will stop traffic?

A: *A school crossing guard uniform.*

Q: Is there anyone over age 50 who still looks great in leotards?

A: *Yes: Superman.*

Q: Where do 50-year-olds look to find fashionable eyeglasses?

A: *Their foreheads.*

Q: Should a 50-year-old consider cosmetic surgery to remove forehead wrinkles?

A: *That might raise a few eyebrows.*

Chapter 5

Recreation

Q: Why don't 50-year-olds mow their lawns?

A: *It's too difficult to steer a riding mower around all the lawn ornaments.*

Q: Is it possible to learn a new language at 50?

A: *Not only is it possible, it's necessary if you plan to buy your first computer.*

Q: What is the most common question that 50-year-olds ask at restaurants?

A: *"Are you sure that's decaffeinated coffee?"*

Q: Who is Elvis Costello?

A: *If you imagine a guy in a white jump suit singing "Viva Las Vegas," you are over 50. If you think of Bud Abbott's partner, you are way over 50.*

Q: What is the most common remark made by 50-year-olds when they enter antique stores?

A: *"I remember these."*

Q: Are cruises just for older people?

A: *Absolutely not. Some people bring along their grandchildren.*

Q: What do all 50-year-olds agree on when it comes to movies?

A: *The remake is never as good as the original.*

Q: Today's films are rated G, PG, PG-13, R, and NC-17. What were they rated a generation or so ago?

A: *Disney, B, and stag.*

Q: What TV celebrity still looks as good as he did 40 years ago?

A: *Howdy Doody.*

Q: Why can going to a baseball game be a sobering experience for a 50-year-old?

A: *You'll probably know more about the players in the Old-Timers Game than you'll know about the regular ball players.*

Q: Is there an outdoor sports club for tough guys who have slowed down with age?

A: *Try Hell's Anglers.*

Q: What's the most important thing to remember about planning a 50th birthday party?

A: *Keep the cake away from the smoke alarm.*

Q: How many pushups should a healthy 50-year-old be able to do?

A: *30 or 31. In February, 28.*

Q: How can you get a 50-year-old to go to bed at 9:00 P.M.?

A: *Give him a 7:00 A.M. tee time.*

Q: Why is bowling a popular sport among 50-year-olds?

A: *You never have to move more than 10 feet at a time; the clothes are comfortable; and the ball rolls back to you.*

103

Q: What are the triathlon events for 50-year-old executives?

A: *Running for the bus, treading water at work, and exercising stock options.*

Q: When is the best time to visit Paris?

A: *Before you get any older.*

Q: When do 50-year-olds become interested in bird watching?

A: *When they first notice crow's-feet.*

Q: What do you call someone who has known 50 years of futility and disappointment?

A: *A Chicago Cubs fan.*

Q: What is a 50-year-old's idea of morning exercise?

A: *Making the coffee stronger.*

Q: How does a 50-year-old stay on top of the news?

A: *By falling asleep on the newspaper.*

Q: Why aren't there more 50-year-old Jeopardy champions?

A: *There's no category called "things you used to know."*

Q: What does "afternoon delight" mean to a 50-year-old?

A: *A nap after lunch.*

Q: What investment advice can a 50-year-old offer to young people?

A: *Never sell the car you owned in high school. No matter what condition the car is in, it will become a classic.*

Chapter 6

Work

Q: Is it possible these days to take early retirement and still live comfortably?

A: *With careful financial planning you can retire 10 years early, provided that you had originally expected to work until age 75.*

Q: What job entitlements should a 50-year-old worker with lots of experience expect?

A: *If you get laid off, you will be entitled to file an age-discrimination lawsuit.*

Q: When it's cold and snowy, 50-year-olds often fantasize that a young stranger will come to their door and say what three magic words?

A: *"Shovel your driveway?"*

Q: What are a few things that a 50-year-old employee should avoid saying, so as not to appear out of touch with today's workplace?

A: *Never say any of the following:*
"Where's the typewriter?"
"What's a cubicle?" "Cute outfit!"

Q: How many career changes should you expect to have by age 50?

A: *If you've switched careers more times than you've switched barbers, you've had too many jobs.*

Q: Are there any professions or social positions for which 50 is the minimum age?

A: *Indeed, there are many: grande dame, dowager, patriarch or matriarch, senior statesman, professor emeritus, and Seniors Tour golfer.*

Q: What words would you prefer to hear from a 50-year-old than from a 30-year-old?

A: *"This is your captain speaking."*